SHĀNTI

Peace of Mind Through Selective Verses

Hari Datt Sharma

V&S PUBLISHERS

Published by:

V&S PUBLISHERS

F-2/16, Ansari Road, Daryaganj, New Delhi-110002
☎ 011-23240026, 011-23240027 • *Fax:* 011-23240028
Email: info@vspublishers.com • *Website:* www.vspublishers.com

Branch : Hyderabad
5-1-707/1, Brij Bhawan (Beside Central Bank of India Lane)
Bank Street, Koti, Hyderabad - 500 095
☎ 040-24737290
E-mail: vspublishershyd@gmail.com

Branch Office : Mumbai
Jaywant Industrial Estate, 2nd Floor–222, Tardeo Road
Opposite Sobo Central Mall, Mumbai – 400 034
☎ 022-23510736
E-mail: vspublishersmum@gmail.com

Follow us on:

All books available at **www.vspublishers.com**

Printed at : Repro Knowledgecast Limited, Thane

Contents

	A Message from the Author	5
	Peace of Mind	7
1.	Why I Write on Peace of Mind	11
2.	Prelude to Peace of Mind	12
3.	From *Ishawasya Upanishad*	13
4.	From *Ishawasya Upanishad*	14
5.	From *Ishawasya Upanishad*	15
6.	From *Ishawasya Upanishad*	16
7.	From *Ishawasya Upanishad*	17
8.	Rama Krishna Says	18
9.	From the *Bhagavad Gita*	19
10.	Rama Krishna Says	20
11.	From the *Bhagavad Gita*	21
12.	God	22
13.	From *Bhagavad Gita*	23
14.	Lord Buddha's Prescription	24
15.	Spiritual Way of Life	25
16.	Count Blessings, Not Troubles	28
17.	Don't Fight With the Inevitable	29
18.	Prayer Can Do Wonders	30
19.	Real Bliss	32
20.	God is One and Only One You Must Understand	33
21.	Rama Krishna Says	35
22.	A Talk Between Yajanvalkya and His Wife Maitreyi	36
23.	A Message From Dhammapad on Buddhism	39
24.	Improve Your Worldly Wisdom Through *Hitopodesha*	40
25.	What is Special in *Bhagavad Gita*	54
26.	Sayings of The Wise Men On Peace of Mind	60

A Message from the Author

The purpose of this book is to restate and glorify a lot of ancient and basic truths about peace of mind and make you do something about applying them. I have written this book mainly in "Elated Prose Style" to help you enjoy it like poetry as well as prose. You didn't pick up this book to know how it was written. You are looking for action. So, please read a few pages carefully and if by that time you don't feel that you are acquiring a new power and a new inspiration to change your lifestyle then toss this book away. It is not good for you.

Peace of mind is the biggest problem facing mankind. Most of the religious books are based on this presumption. Hurry and worry, stress and strain are the modern enemies of peace. These must have to be subdued to protect oneself from diseases like Heart Attack, High BP, Diabetes, Ulcer, and Cancer etc. People are dying like flies due to these diseases.

Read each page rapidly at first to get a bird's-eye view of it. But if you are determined to attain peace of mind, then go back and re-read each page thoroughly. Stop frequently in your reading to think over what you are reading. Try to understand each idea. That kind of reading will aid you far more than racing ahead like a hound chasing a fox. After reading, review every page in your mind after closing your eyes.

Whatever you have read in this book, try to find out, how it can be applied in real life, otherwise you will forget it quickly. Only knowledge that is used sticks in our mind.

I am indebted to all those authors whose books inspired me and enabled me to write this book. My special gratitudes are to Dale Carnegie and Sweat Morden whose books encouraged me and prepared my mind to move towards peace of mind. I am also very thankful to His Holiness Late Swami Shivananda Ji and many other authors whose writings moved me towards peace of mind. I am not a learned man. My knowledge of English language is limited. This book is the end product of my deep studies.

I wish all of you peace of mind.

Hari Datt Sharma
Organiser
Peace of Mind Mission.

PEACE OF MIND

What is peace of mind? Is it possible to attain peace of mind? These questions often baffle many people, who have no clear conception of peace of mind. Peace of mind does not mean soothing the mind. It does not mean escape into a dream world. It means more effective participation in a real world. It does not mean innocuous lulling but dynamic stimulation of creative activity. Peace of mind greatly increases our intellectual power. It enables us to think rationally and in a better way. An excited mind can not produce rational concept or orderly thoughts. The mind is efficient only when it is cool and not hot. When our mind is heated, emotions control our judgement which proves costly in the long run. Power of the mind comes from the quietness. Nothing is as precious as peace of mind. Peace of mind is the peaceful base upon which we erect a good deal of life dynamic. Money can buy many things but not peace of mind. Nothing can bring you peace but yourself. To have peace of mind one has to discipline oneself never to get mad or resentful. It is very important to learn emotional management.

Most of the religious books emphasize to keep under control vices like lust, anger, greed, hatred, envy, jealousy and ill will etc., which are the main enemies of peace of mind. In the Gita Lord Krishna says—

Lust, anger and greed are the triple gates of the hell,

These take the person towards the hell.

Hurry, worry, stress and strain are the modern enemies. These enemies destroy peace of mind and produce diseases in the body. Heart troubles, ulcer, nervous breakdown like maladies are caused by these enemies of peace.

Many psychosomatic diseases like insomnia, constant fatigue, impotency, headache, indigestion etc., are caused due to unpeace of mind.

There is a right and a wrong way to do everything. There is also a right and a wrong way to live life. Living is also a science based on definite laws of nature. Those who do not cooperate with laws of nature, life goes badly. When you learn those laws and live within them, your life will be wonderful.

A person who has self control, has strength to see situations clearly. Judge them for what they are. It depends upon the attitude of your mind. Negative attitude disturbs and positive attitude provides peace to the mind.

Little things in life drive people to the edge of insanity and cause many troubles and headache. Trivialities are at the bottom of most of the marital unhappiness. Domestic wrangling, an insulting remark, a disparaging word, a rude action, false display of wealth, false display of boldness are the little things that lead to assault and murders. The small man flies into rage over the slightest criticism, but the wise man is always eager to learn from those who have censured him and reproved him.

Sharing of happiness brings happiness when the sharing is voluntary, with no other object than to give.

When we try to please others, we stop thinking of ourselves. This is the very thing that protects us from worry, fear and melancholia. Serving the people without any motive makes them beam with pleasure. According to the Gita—

"With ill will and egoism, you can't be a true devotee,

Compassion is the main sign of a true devotee.
People of doubting nature can't get happiness,
Only faith and wisdom can provide happiness."

Those who do not know how to relax are slow poisoning their body. You must know how to relax your body to avoid fatigue of body and mind.

But peace of mind which you hunt outside is within you. All the worries and miseries are the creations of your mind. By changing your attitude you can easily change them.

Wealth, beauty, name, fame, prosperity and power all fail to satisfy man's inner craving. As a last resort he turns his attention within and finds there the fountain of happiness. Everybody likes peace.

Why I Write on Peace of Mind

You would like to know why I write on peace of mind?
How Peace of Mind Mission can help to attain peace of
*   mind?*
My answer is very simple and straight,
Some time tested recipes I want to state.

Life is very miserable and troublesome these days,
We have to face tension & financial troubles these days.
It has become difficult to keep pace with life,
All are feeling helpless may be a husband or a wife.

Hurry & worry, Stress and strain are giving us troubles,
And are causing cardiac, gastric and respiratory troubles.
Anxiety is producing signs of many diseases,
Heart attack, diabetes and stomach pain like diseases.

People are feeling helpless and dying like flies,
These are destroying many valuable lives.
Main cause of all these maladies is un-peace of mind.
Enemies of peace are disturbing the mind.

Most of the diseases are only psychosomatic,
Peace of mind is the tool of remedy and pragmatic.
If you want to get rid of all these maladies,
Peace of mind is the answer to fight these maladies.

Money can buy many things but not peace of mind,
That is why I dare to write on peace of mind.
I am a humble volunteer of Peace of Mind Mission,
To help you to attain peace is my sole mission.

Prelude to Peace of Mind

This book may guide you to attain peace of mind,
But it is only you who yourself can find.
None can physically help you to attain peace of mind,
As it solely depends upon your own inner mind.

Stress, strain and worry are the main problems these days,
Heart attack is the biggest killer in these days.
Peace of mind does not mean soothing state of mind,
But to provide a great source of energy to the mind.

It is not an escape into a dream world,
But effective participation in a real world.
It is not like innocuous lulling of a person,
But to make a dynamic and stimulating person.

It greatly increases intellectual power of mind,
A cool mind is more efficient than a hot mind.
In a hot mind emotions control the judgement,
In a cool mind moral laws control the judgement.

It can also remove sense of guilt from the mind,
Only then peace can enter and stay in the mind.
I am not telling anything new, you already did not know,
Many golden rules to get peace of mind, you also know.

Let me point out towards your ignorance and inaction,
And to restate a few basic truths to take some action.
All my recipes are time tested to attain peace of mind,
If you pick even a few, you will notice change in your mind.

From *Ishawasya Upanishad**

Though I am sinful, yet there is no difference in me and
Him (God)
I am He, and a part of Him.
This body is a covering over the essential me,
If one can pierce through the body can catch a glimpse of
Thee.

From *Ishawasya Upanishad*

It is wrong to desire to live without doing work in life,
Covetousness is caused due to desire to live an easy life.
Live your life by carrying on incessant work,
Life becomes a burden when one always shirks off work.

People suffer when they act in that way,
Much of the sins in the world are due to the desire to live in easy
  way.

From *Ishawasya Upanishad*

All kind of knowledge is not at all needed,
Only some kind of knowledge in life is needed.
One must learn what kind of knowledge is required,
And what kind of knowledge is not required.

Life remains disturbed by useless knowledge,
Will also remain disturbed due to lack of knowledge.

From *Ishwasya Upanishad*

Those who forget God and hunt for pleasure seeking life,
Spurn the dignity of labour and lead an easy life,
Destroy their potential finer self,
And pave the way for the hell themselves.

Man has built many barriers between man and man,
It is causing strife in society, state, family and in man,
This can be eliminated with the true knowledge of God,
But only a true devotee can get this fruit from the God.

From *Ishawasya Upanishad*

Knowledge is necessary as well as ignorance,
What is not necessary, let that remain in ignorance.
If useless knowledge had been acquired that should be
            forgotten,
Don't pay any heed, let it should be rotten.

By following it, the wisdom becomes centred in God,
By not following it, one goes away from the God.
Knowledge and ignorance are part and parcel of life,
But some kind of knowledge is a must to become successful in
            life.

Rama Krishna Says

The world is full of temptation, mind can break discipline,
But perfect man is that whose mind is under discipline.
A mud fish lives in muddy water but is not soiled,
This world is like muddy water, learn to live without getting
soiled.

From the *Bhagavad Gita**

What you are holding will not be yours by tomorrow,
You got it from others, will go to others by morrow.
What happened or happening is for the better,
In future also will happen for the better.

Change is the continuing process of the world,
Changes are taking place every moment in the world.
What you see now, may not be by tomorrow in the world,
Going going gone, is the rule of the world.

Rama Krishna Says

Accumulated riches meet the fate of a bee hive,
Bees themselves never eat their own honey, but others loot the
     hive.
There are many who can give very good advice,
But there are only a few who care to follow a good advice.

From *Bhagavad Gita*

Why crying? What have you lost in the world?
What is now yours, was with any other in the world.
You brought nothing, will take away nothing from here,
What you have lost was taken from here.

God

God is hidden inside your heart,
To find Him open the door of your heart.
As musk is hidden inside the deer,
But wanders here and there as is not clear.

God is also hidden inside the heart.
Remove your ignorance and see Him in your heart.

From *Bhagavad Gita*

Thou has a right only on your actions,
Thou has no right on the fruit of those actions.
Do all actions without attachment or motive,
The fruit of action should not be thy motive.

Do your work in a spirit of great sacrifice,
Perform your duty without attachment or price.
Craving and anger impel to do the sins,
Those who have gained wisdom can avoid those sins.

Lord Buddha's Prescription

None can seek happiness through hurting others,
Happiness comes only when you love others.
You yourself fear death and fear pain,
Then why do you kill or cause others any pain.

Don't use harsh words and provoke others,
They may also pay you back in the same coin may be your
            brother.
Then it will produce anger in your mind,
And sufferings will follow of strange kinds.

Do as you wish to be done by,
Its the golden rule of the wise.
A person should not live heedlessly,
But should exert to live righteously.

Spiritual Way of Life

It is not very difficult to lead a spiritual life,
One has to make some adjustments in one's daily life.
No need to follow any specific religion,
As inner attitude is important than following any religion.

One has to acquire insight into the realities of the world,
How conflicting forces like good and evil are affecting the
*   world.*
All these are intertwined in the social fabric of the society,
One must appreciate the diversities found in the society.

One has to learn to play one's role in the society,
By contributing constructive and selfless services for the
*   society.*
Start your day in a dynamic and spiritual way,
By doing meditation regularly every day.

Concentrate upon the meaning of God as the dynamic world
*   spirit,*
With truth, freedom, welfare, creative action, try to realize
*   your spirit.*
Make a mental survey of all the activities you propose to do
*   that day,*
Rehearse within yourself how best you can do that day.

Perform them in accordance with the spiritual ideal of life,
Don't allow your daily schedule to be over-crowded in life.
Select carefully the important matters just enough for the
*   day,*
Set aside other things for the next day.

Perform those actions in the attitude of serving the divine.
For one's own self, society and the will of the divine.
Whenever you find a little free time in the course of the
*   day,*
Rededicate yourself as an instrument of the divine at least once
*   a day.*

Repeat the name of your God in your own mind,
You will feel divine protection in your mind.
Before retiring at night do a reflection or meditation,
Offering thanks to God for your good luck and recreation.

Such a spirit of thanksgiving would prevent vanity and
*   pride,*
Would prove a source of encouragement and without anything
*   to hide.*
Remembrance of God transmutes egotism into self esteem,
Encourages to adopt only fair and proper means.

Then make a comprehensive and critical review of activities of
*   the day,*
For some you may feel proud, for some you may feel sorry
*   that day.*
Don't allow your feelings to sour your life,
Find out what mistakes were made, to prevent them in
*   future life.*

After extracting lessons of the day, banish all thoughts from
*   the mind,*
Adopt a relaxed attitude and establish perfect silence in
*   mind.*
When you will adopt this kind of prayful attitude,
You will get a sound sleep, with that attitude.

God has bestowed man an innate faculty of knowledge,
One can discover the truth with that knowledge.

Count Blessings, Not Troubles

People often count their troubles, never count their blessings,
Troubles are very few in comparison with the blessings.
For our troubles we often complain to God,
But for boons and bounties we never thank God.

Think of the man who has no eyes or legs,
Think of the man who always begs,
Compare yourself with such unfortunate people,
Is not God more generous with you than those people?

People seldom think of what they have,
They always complain of what they do not have.
These kinds of thinking always disturb the mind,
And make it difficult to attain peace of mind.

Fortunes and misfortunes are the part and parcel of life,
Try to adjust yourself accordingly in your life.
What can't be cured must be endured, always keep in mind,
Accept it as the will of God and don't disturb your mind.

Every cloud has a silver lining too,
Only patience can bring comforts to you.
First count your blessings, then count your troubles,
Then you can face boldly all your troubles.

Don't Fight With The Inevitable

Don't worry what is hidden in the store of your future,
Who knows what will happen in the future?
Do your work as best as you can do,
Don't worry what is written in the fate for you.

This is the main teaching of the Gita,
It was said by Lord Krishna to Arjuna in the Gita.
The future is affected by many forces,
None can tell who prompts all those forces.

Don't worry about things which are beyond your power,
Leave those things to the Almighty God's power.
When one stops fighting with the inevitable,
One creates new energy to face that inevitable.

Bend like the willow; don't resist like the oak,
This is a reality which many wise men spoke.
What can't be cured must be endured is the rule divine,
When you can do nothing, why do you mind.

Life is an index of our inner thoughts,
Happiness or misery is felt due to those thoughts.
One feels happy with positive attitude,
One feels sad with negative attitude.

Prayer Can Do Wonders

Prayer is the most powerful form of energy,
Like Radium it also produces luminous and self generating
energy.
When one prays one links itself with the inexhaustible motive
power,
Universe is being run by that power.

We seek to augment that finite energy,
By addressing ourselves to that finite source of energy.
Whenever we address God in fervent prayer,
Our body and mind feel better after that prayer.

Only faith and God can help us to utilize our hidden energy,
Without his inspiration none can awaken that energy.
Prayer can help all types of persons,
One may be a theist or an atheist person.

When all types of therapy had badly failed,
Through sincere prayers any body can hail.
Prayer helps to put into words what is troubling our mind,
It is like understanding the problem that is hurting our
mind.

One can discuss with God even the most secret problems,
And can feel relaxed after sharing those problems.
Prayer encourages us to take some actions,
Then we feel peace as a reaction.

Pent up energy releases, when one says prayer,
Incurable diseases can be cured with the prayer.
That is why all the religions greatly emphasize to say regular
prayer,

Panacea for many troubles is the sincere prayer.

Don't say your prayers just as a formality,
Pray from the core of your heart, not as a formality.

Real Bliss

Real bliss is being guarded by a five hooded serpent,
Our own mind itself is that five hooded serpent.
It hisses through its five senses to divert our attention,
From the real bliss it keeps away our attention.
None can attain real happiness without taming that serpent,
Lord Krishna was able to tame that serpent.

God is One and Only One
You Must Understand

You were born a boy or a girl, not a man of religion,
You were made to believe yourself man of any religion.
When he was born the nurse said, "A boy is born".
When she was born the nurse said, "A girl is born".

Your parents labelled you in the religion of their own,
That is why many kinds of religions are known.
Religions were made, to tell the people, how to worship God,
Religions were made, to tell the people, have faith in God.

Religions were made, to tell the people, how to make amends,
But people are using religions, to meet their selfish ends.
Many wars and battles were fought, in the name of religion,
Many people were butchered and maimed, in the name of
*   religion.*

Many people are being exploited, in the name of religion,
Many people are being befooled, in the name of religion.
Religions teach us, love mankind, not to hate and fight,
Religions teach us, help the poors, not to exploit their rights.

Religions teach us, make the society useful and bright,
Religions teach us, shun violence always be polite.
Different religions are different ways, to worship the same
*   God,*
By hating any other religion you are insulting your own
*   God.*

Religion is a private matter, why not take this stand,
To save the people from brutal killings on this very land.
God lives in his creations on this very land,

First God is your mother, then your motherland.
Your work is also worship you must understand,
To shirk work is a treachery of the motherland.
To help the poor and helpless is true worship on land,
This is the only universal religion, you must understand.

You were born a boy or a girl not a man of religion.
You were made to believe yourself man of any religion.

Rama Krishna Says

There should be harmony between your thoughts and speech,
Only then your message in the heart of others can reach.
Those who are simple can attain the God,
Thief of their own thoughts can't attain the God.
One who does any thing only for sake of show,
He is very cunning person very very low.

A Talk Between Yajañvalkya and His Wife Maitreyi

Yajanvalkya had Katyani and Maitreyi, two lovely wives,
Katyani was worldly, while Maitreyi was spiritually wise.
When Yajanvalkya decided to renounce the world,
To acquire true knowledge of the world.

He approached his wife Maitreyi for her consent,
And to divide his wealth between both, with their mutual
        consent,
But Maitreyi refused to accept any wealth,
Because immortality cannot be gained with the wealth.

O dear husband! if you really love me,
Whatever you know about Brahma please tell me.
O dear Maitreyi! you were always very dear to me,
Your question is also a favourite of me.

Please listen to me with attentive mind,
And try to understand it with your mind.
A husband is not dear for the sake of husband but for one's
        own self,
A wife is not dear for the sake of wife but for one's own
        self.

A son is not dear for son's sake but for the sake of the self,
Wealth is not dear for the sake of wealth but for the own
        self.
All are dear not for all but for the sake of the self,
Everybody likes to satisfy one's own self.

Therefore self should be seen, heard and contemplated upon,
Self is very dear to us, so it should be meditated upon.

When one plays any musical instrument,
Ears grasp only one tune of different tunes of that instrument.

After inner knowledge all sounds seem to give one tune,
Ears of the mind then listen only one tune.
After appropriate knowledge Brahma can be felt everywhere,
As dissolved salt can't be seen but may be felt in water
        everywhere.

It is out of atma (soul) that everything else springs,
In him everything lives and everything dissolves in him.
When the senses feel duality in our mind,
Only then one can see, smell, hear and speak of other kinds.

But when the self merges into the soul and becomes one,
All the duality ceases and one becomes only one.
Existence of the world can't be known without atma (soul),
To explain the existence of the world it is a must to know
        atma.

As smoke gives indication of the existence of fire,
No smoke is possible without the fire.
Similarly world is an indication of the existence of Brahma,
There might be any creator of this world, who is none else but
        Brahma.

When the world is dissolved by Brahma,
Everything dissolves except the consciousness of Brahma.
In this life you are subject to hunger, thirst, birth and death,
After knowing you will dissolve into Brahma who is without
        fear of birth and death.

Consciousness that is born out of Avidya (ignorance),
Of the complex of body, senses and mind is destroyed with

Vidya.
Brahma is the Atma of all beings,
And does not perish with the perish of all beings.

A Message From Dhammapad*
on Buddhism

Do good deeds and sow good seeds,
Evil deeds evil breed.
When you make anybody happy, happiness you sow,
When you make anybody unhappy, unhappiness you sow.

When you do cruel things, you sow cruelty,
Afterwards it grows up into cruelty.
When you do kindness, kindness you sow,
When you do cheating, cheating you grow.

When you yourself don't like death or to suffer pain,
Why are you giving to others death or pain.
Whatever you sow, so you reap,
Good or bad you yourself heap.

Desires breed misery you must understand,
Keep them in check if you can.

Rust
Rust and evil deeds do the same action,
One eats the iron, other eats the body as a reaction.
To save the iron from the rust some paint is needed,
To save the body from the rust good deeds are needed.

Death
One who is born must have to die,
Birth is certain for those who have died,
Cycle of birth and death is inevitable,
Only God has the power to make it alterable.

* An ancient Buddhist Monk.

Improve Your Worldly Wisdom Through *Hitopodesha*

Hitopodesha is the most popular and famous Sanskrit book which had already inspired and is still inspiring many people. It had been translated in many languages of the world. Everything is explained through comprehensive and simple animal stories. The listeners are expected to grasp the moral of the story themselves. It is one of the oldest methods of teaching when textbooks were not available. The hand-written books were used to teach the children of the kings, nobles and rich families. It was a story-telling method. After telling the story, the moral was wound up in a Sanskrit shloka. The students were expected to learn that shloka by heart.

I have translated main ideas of a few of those shlokas into English Couplets. I am sure readers will enjoy it and may like to read it again and again. All the couplets are full of worldly knowledge and wisdom to become a wise person in the society. All the couplets directly touch our heart as those are related to real life situations of our day to day life.

1.
What is the advantage of eyes to a blind man,
What is the advantage of a foolish son to a wise man.

2.
A son unborn or dead causes grief for a short time,
But a foolish son causes grief for a long time.

3.
One wise son is better than one hundred foolish sons,
To remove the darkness there is only one Sun.

4.

Health, wealth, loving wife and obedient children,
These gifts of God are available only to a few ones.

5.

Attachment to money and life is strong in human life,
But to an old man his young wife is more dear than his
own life.

6.

People use sweet words when there is any motive,
A young wife hugs her old husband when there is any
motive.

7.

In indigestion food works as a poison to a man,
A young wife also proves a poison to an old man.

8.

Eating, sleeping, fear, offsprings are common in all living
things,
Only moral goodness distinguishes human from other living
things.

9.

Life, action, wealth, wisdom and then death,
Is the human destiny from birth to death.

10.

Lazy people believe in fate while wise believe in action,
Where there is an action, there is surely a reaction.

11.

In fine clothes every person appears a gentle person,
Only the speech reveals, of what type is that person.

12.

Avarice can make even a wise person blind,
Although they can see yet not from their mind.

13.

In adversities, mind also becomes very smear,
Even Lord Rama believed in the existence of a golden deer.

14.

One who praises at the face, but abuses at the back,
Is not fit for friendship, as good qualities lack.

15.

Sweet words and pretended services are used to cheat,
These tools are often used by all the cheats.

16.

Friendship should be avoided with the evil nature,
Coal may be hot or cold spoils the hand as per its nature.

17.

Many people flatter at the face but backbite at behind,
When they find any weak point, in harming they never
mind.

18.

When an evil natured person speaks kindly, have no confidence
in him,
His heart is full of poison upto the brim.

19.

Vices get punishment and virtues get reward,
Sooner or later everybody gets its due award.

20.

A woman is like butter, a man is like fire,
It is not wise to put the butter close to the fire.

21.

Poverty and death both give pain,
Pain of death is shortlived, but pain of poverty always
    remains.

22.

It is money which is respected not the person who holds,
As soon as one loses the money, is ignored like an old.

23.

Poverty destroys virtues, old age destroys beauty,
Sunlight destroys darkness, servitude destroys sense of duty.

24.

Food at the expense of others, love bought for money,
These are the miseries, never give a taste like honey.

25.

Delight in poetry, company of virtues in the world,
Are the two sweet fruits on the poisonous tree of the world.

26.

One who hoards money at the cost of happiness,
Neither enjoys money, nor gets happiness.

27.

A miser's life is just like a blacksmith's bellow,
Although he is breathing, yet a wretched fellow.

28.

As a lamp shows nothing to a blind man,
Scriptures have no value for a foolish man.

29.

Pain and pleasure are like two wheels,
Without them our life can not reel.

30.

Even without riches a wise man gains honour,
But even with riches a miser gains dishonour.

31.

Youth, riches, parents and beauty,
Abandon everybody after doing their duty.

32.

Fortunes never favour a lazy slack man,
As a young girl never likes to hug an old man.

33.

Sex, bad health, home sickness and idleness,
Are a few obstacles in the way of greatness.

34.

Appearance, movement, eyes, speech, gestures and gait,
What is in the mind, can clearly indicate.

35.

A crow takes nothing, a cuckoo gives nothing,

Sweet words get appreciation and harsh words get nothing.

36.

For fear of indigestion, none will like to eat nothing,
From fear of mistakes, why do you like to do nothing.

37.

A creeper itself winds around whatever is nearby,
A minister shows favour to the person who is nearby.

38.

Weapon, book, lute, speech of any person,
Their usefulness depends on the use by the person.

39.

A corrupt mind always thinks about evil things,
Shakuni and Shaktare are the proofs of this thing.

40.

Power and riches change every mind,
The owner misconceives that he has a very great mind.

41.

Affections of a wicked person can not be gained,
As from a poisonous tree good fruit can not be obtained.

42.

Secret confidence is like the seed of a plant,
If one breaks it, it can't be used to implant.

43.

An angry person may be pacified, if causes of anger are
removed,
But a person with hostile mind, can not be moved.

44.

To meet their selfish ends, scounderals corrupt a virtuous
        man,
This is the easiest method used by a wicked man.

45.

Mere knowledge of a medicine can't cure disease,
Proper diagnose is a must to eradicate that disease.

46.

A crow is very clever but eats filthy things,
A clever person always miseries brings.

47.

Learning is that eye which clears many doubts,
Reveals many hidden things without any doubt.

48.

Lazy people believe only in their fate,
Diligent neither shirk work nor they hate.

49.

Result of the past deeds is called fate,
So why not work with vigour to make your fate.

50.

To give birth to a son can't make the son wise,
Proper guidance only can make him wise.

51.

Sloth, slumber, fear, anger and postponement,
Are the main obstacles in the way of attainment.

52.

With heavy make-up and fine clothes every woman looks
      pretty,
Only her speech reveals about the type of her beauty.

53.

A frog is never attracted to the lotus, though living nearby,
But a bee runs towards the lotus, though not living nearby.

54.

A virtuous person appreciates virtues in others,
A person who is not good in himself, never cares for others.

55.

When a person of lower mind is raised to an honourable
      post,
Tries to get rid of that person, who helped him to get that
      post.

56.

The parents who fail to give proper education to their children,
Are the worst enemies of their own children.

57.

Avarice is the cause of many misdeeds,
It is the root of many evils, one must take heed.

58.

Cheerfulness in adversity and calmness in prosperity,
Are rarely seen in the humanity.

59.

A dog that has lost teeth, licks a bone to have some taste.

*A helpless old person also likes to enjoy senses to have their
taste.*

60.

*Likeness or dislikeness depends upon enjoymet,
As cattle like to wander anywhere in search of enjoyment.*

61.

*Some women remain unfaithful even among Gods,
Those are very lucky, whose wives are faithful to their lords.*

62.

*A person should conceal age, money, penance and medicine
he takes,
Domestic troubles, private counsels, liberality and his disgrace.*

63.

*Poverty is the root of many evils in the world,
It makes the person to lose self respect in this world.*

64.

*It is better to remain silent than speaking unkind words,
Better to be impotent than philandering in the world.*

65.

*A covetous person never heeds any kind of reason,
Greed always compels not to listen to good reasons.*

66.

*A greedy person can never be made contented,
Even after getting whole world's wealth, remains discontented.*

67.

It is not the money that makes one rich,

It is the contentment that makes one rich.

68.

Those who acquire ill-gotten money can't get peace,
It is the contentment that gives peace.

69.

To get something, a greedy man can travel for many miles,
But a contented person doesn't bother for undue things, even
lying nearby.

70.

Discrimination between good and bad is the real learning,
Money earned through righteous means is the real earning.

71.

Compassion towards all is the real happiness,
Freedom from diseases is the real happiness.

72.

What is the use of money, not given or used,
What is the use of scriptures whose teachings are not used.

73.

A miser's wealth is nothing more, than a piece of stone,
Either it is destroyed or taken away by the persons unknown.

74.

Liberality with kindness, contempt for illegal wealth of all
kinds,
Bravery with forbearance, knowledge with pride,
These are the good qualities, very difficult to find.

75.

The mere name of a drug can't cure disease,
Knowledge without action always cease.

76.

Heaping of the riches gives troubles and not happiness,
Loss of the riches gives sorrow, then how riches can give
happiness.

77.

Keep away from mud than to wash it off,
Keep away from ill-gotten wealth than to pass it off.

78.

A rich man is afraid of fire, thieves, rulers, relatives and all
beings,
As there is a danger of death to all living beings.

79.

Wealth is difficult to acquire and very difficult to keep,
Its loss is very painful, be careful when wealth you seek.

80.

To visit without invitation, to speak without being asked,
To think oneself valuable to one's master is a foolish task.

81.

Mind your own business is a good advice,
Before meddling in anyone's affairs think it thrice.

82.

Success or failure are the ways of life,
Bear them happily to lead a happy life.

83.

Incapacity causes misfortunes, expedient causes prosperity,
A wise person can change his adversity into prosperity.

84.

One can wear a piece of glass on hand, and on foot can wear a
jewel,
But as value is concerned, a glass is a glass and a jewel is a
jewel.

85.

One who is respected by the ruler is respected by all,
Degraded by the ruler is despised by all.

86.

If one can't overpower an insignificant enemy,
Put forward an opponent to seize that enemy.

87.

The hurricane never hurts grass, which is not mighty,
It uproots only lofty trees, as a mighty fights a mighty.

88.

A squanderer loses everything after some time,
May be holding billions at a particular time.

89.

Wood can't satisfy the fire, rivers can't satisfy the ocean,
Beauty can't be satisfied after millions of adorations.

90.

One who does not lose heart at unexpected events,
Can easily win over all such events.

91.

As poisonous herbs and loose teeth are quickly removed,
Evil minister should also be quickly removed.

92.

Everyone desires fortunes and admires beauty,
Everybody looks with longing on the young beauty.

93.

Don't punish anybody without investigation,
Information of others may prove wrong after investigation.

94.

To reward or punish without considering merits or faults,
Is like to play with a lion who may tear apart.

95.

A drowning man if lays hold of a serpent,
Can neither hold on, nor let go that serpent.

96.

Roots are full of snakes, flowers are full of bees,
Branches are full of monkeys, that is the fate of a sandal
    tree.

97.

To quarrel with the family, to adopt improper business,
To contend with stronger, to disclose secret of any kind,
Always leads towards a downfall, keep it in mind.

98.

A villain carries corruption wherever he goes,
Ravana carried away Sita ignoring his vow.

99.

Don't contest with anybody before knowing his strength,
Otherwise you will have to lose all your strength.

100.

Youth, beauty, life, riches, power and friends,
Pass away quickly without any amends.

101.

Fear from the danger when it is at a distance,
Face it bravely, when not at a distance.

102.

As the same person forms many relations in this world,
So, many thorns of sorrow he plants in this world.

103.

Receive a friend with kindness, a relative with affectionate
haste,
Servants and women with gifts and honour without being
late.

What is Special in *Bhagavad Gita*

The Gita is the knowledge of Almighty Power,
Krishna gave to Arjuna in difficult hours.
It is the science of the Absolute God,
Scripture of the Yoga to find that God.

It is a part of the battle of Mahabharat,
Kauravas Pandavas fought this battle of Mahabharat.
Wise men never grieve for the dead or alive,
Thou remained and will remain in any life.

The souls go on changing from one to another form,
Existent will not cease; non-existent will not born.
As a person casts off worn out clothes,
Puts on new clothes discarding old clothes.

Souls also cast off worn out bodies,
And again enter in new bodies.
Water, weapon, wind, fire can't cleave the soul,
Uncleavable and eternal is the soul.

It is all pervading, fire can't burn it,
Wind can't dry it, water can't wet it.
One who is born must have to die,
Birth is certain for those who have died.

Cycle of birth and death is inevitable,
Only realisation of Brahma can make it alterable.
Thou has a right only on your actions,
Thou has no right on the fruit of those actions.
Do all actions without attachment or motive,
The fruit of actions should not be thy motive.

In sorrow and pleasure if one has untroubled mind,
Passion, fear, rage have passed away from the mind.

You are like a sage of well settled mind,
Can attain the God with the control of mind.
Draw away the senses from the objects of senses,
As a tortoise withdraws his organs of senses.

Objects of senses give birth to attachment,
Desires are produced due to those attachments.
Then in turn anger and bewilderness is produced,
Destruction of intelligence is also produced.

Attachment, aversion can be controlled with the control of
         mind,
Then thou can control sorrows of many kinds.
Desires, longings, egoism disturb peace of mind,
Running after senses always disturbs peace of mind.

Mere control of senses without the control of mind,
Is a hypocrisy of very strange kind.
Do your work in a spirit of great sacrifice.
Perform your duty without attachment or price,

Craving and anger impell to do the sins,
Only with the wisdom you can avoid such sins.
People of doubting nature can't get happiness,
Only faith and wisdom can provide happiness.

Those who firmly believe in God,
Are only able to seek the God.
Knowledge is better than mere concentration,
But better than knowledge is the meditation.

Better than meditation is renunciation,
Peace may be gained with the renunciation.
With ill will and egoism you can't be a true devotee,
Compassion is the main sign of a true devotee.

Even minded in pain and pleasure is a true devotee,
Who has no lust, anger, greed is the true devotee.
Satav, Rajas, Tamas, Gunas are the three modes,
Goodness, passion and dullness are these modes.

Goodness produces happiness, passion produces actions,
Dullness gives ignorance as a reaction.
From goodness arises knowledge, from the passion greed,
From the dullness negligence always breeds.

When the body rises above these modes of life,
Is freed from birth and death, attains eternal life.
Satviks eat balanced food must for life,
Rajasics like tasty foods for enjoyment in life.

Tamasics like stale foods useless for life,
As per their nature they eat and drink in life.
Demonic nature has ostentation and arrogance,
Pride, anger, harshness and ignorance.

Neither they know way of action nor renunciation,
Neither purity, good conduct nor good actions.
Due to ignorance some feel they are very mighty,
Due to their wealth and power they feel they are mighty.
Due to money and muscles they believe they are powerful,
Can make anybody bow before their will.
Their only aim is to gratify their desires,
Always try to fulfil insatiable desires.

Amass hoards of wealth by unjust means,
Happily they apply all foul means.
Such people drag themselves towards the hell,
Due to bad deeds can't avoid the hell.

They take re-birth in the demonic families.
Or take birth in the lower creatures families.
Divine nature are fearless and pure in mind,
Have charity, sacrifice, austerity and control of mind.

Uprightness, non-violence, truth and forgiveness,
Tranquillity, compassion, modesty and gentleness.
Good men worship only the real Gods,
Passionate persons worship even the demi Gods.

Dull people worship spirits and ghosts,
To fulfil hidden desires they worship these ghosts.
Happiness from pure heart is the real happiness,
Objects of senses can't give the real happiness.

Sleep and sloth can't give real happiness,
Knowledge of the soul only can give real happiness.
Passions produce lust and lust produces anger,
Insatiable like fire is the lust and anger.

Lust, anger and greed are the gates to the hell,
These take the person towards the hell.
When people of demonic nature increase on the earth,
To wipe them off God descends on the earth.

To protect the nobles and punish the ignobles,
To remind values of life which are very noble.
People can worship God in any name and form,
He comes to them in the same name and form.

He never minds how you call Him,
Is ready to come in what every way you call Him.
What is now your, was with others in the past,
Why weeping you had lost nothing at last.

What you are holding will not be yours by tomorrow,
You got it from others, will go to others by morrow.
What happened or happening may be for the better,
In future also, will happen for the better.

Change is the continuous process in the world,
Going, going, gone is the rule of the world,
You brought nothing will take nothing from here,
What you have lost, was taken from here.

Pain and pleasure don't last for ever,
Only this reality will prevail for ever.
When one likes any object intimacy is produced,
Out of intimacy, desire to seek is produced.

When there is obstruction, anger is produced,
Due to that anger confusion is produced.
Due to that confusion power of reasoning is destroyed,
Then destruction of the man none can avoid.
But the man whose internal sense is under control,
Can enjoy happiness, keeping mind under control.
Senses, Mind and Reasons dwell in the body,
Can very easily confuse any body.

Mind is beyond senses, Reason is beyond Mind,
Atman (soul) is beyond reason, Senses may be controlled with
      the mind.

Who has no hate desire is the true ascetic,
Although doing Karma yet a true ascetic.

Karma Yoga and Sankhya are the similar paths,
Meet at the same spot both these paths.
Mind like wind can't be controlled,
But through practice and vairagya can be controlled.

When with practice one steadies the mind,
Through meditation even Him can find.
One who eats nothing or eats too much,
One who keeps awake or sleeps too much.

Can not succeed in attaining Yoga,
Who eats sleeps just sufficient, can attain Yoga.
Desires never satisfy by the enjoyment,
Goes on increasing after every enjoyment.

Desire is the constant enemy of the learned man,
Envelops the knowledge of the man.
Om-Tat-Sat is the root of the Universe,
By uttering these words, Brahma created Universe.

It is very simple even a child can recite,
It has immense power, you can also recite.

Sayings of The Wise Men
On Peace of Mind

1. *Money can buy many things but not peace of mind. It is only you who yourself can find.*
2. *Nothing can bring you peace but your self.*
3. *It is the forgetfulness of the "I-ness" which fills the person with happiness or gives pleasure. To lose oneself is to find oneself.*
4. *The peace of Mind which you hunt outside is hidden within you. All the worries and miseries are the creations of your own mind. By changing your attitude you can easily change them.*
5. *Like a cocoon, you are always weaving threads of thoughts, which keep you imprisoned, involved or enveloped, never allowing a restful moment. Only sleep gives it a little pause.*
6. *Wealth, beauty, name, fame, prosperity, and power, all fail to satisfy man's inner cravings. As a last resort, he turns his attention within and finds there the fountain of happiness.*
7. *A person who can control himself can move the world. Self is that point where the lever of the Archimedes can be placed to lift the world.*
8. *The secret of happiness is hidden in the proper and rightful use of the senses, mind, money and time.*
9. *God has not made anything without any purpose, however tiny, filthy or valueless an object may appear.*
10. *It is not the fault of senses, mind, money or leisure. When we misuse them we encounter difficulties and troubles. These are made to serve you. But their use or misuse is in your own hands.*
11. *Renunciation is from mind. We do not live where our bodies live. We live where our minds live. Solitude can be had at home or it can not be had in remotest forest. (Swami Ram Tirath)*

12. *Money itself is not an enemy. Money is needed at every step. Money can be an excellent aid to progress whether spiritual, mental or material.*

13. *A man does not become an ascetic by merely giving up actions because of laziness, ignorance or hardship of work. An ascetic is one who is endowed with necessary knowledge and practises self discipline and self control.*

14. *According to the Udgith of the Chandogya Upanishad—*
    Earth is the essence of elements,
    Water is the essence of the earth,
    Plants are the essence of water,
    Flowers are the essence of plants,
    Fruits are the essence of flowers,
    Man is the essence of fruits,
    Semen is the seed of the man,
    Speech is the essence of the man.

    Semen is the seed of the man. It is the seed that develops into a tree. Loss of semen results in irritability and anger in temperament. Semen is the source of life. Many insects die after sexual intercourse. One sexual act releases 120 calories of heat, which is equal to the heat produced after running fast for one kilometre or the amount of energy spent in physical labour for ten days, or mental work performed during three days. Excessive loss of semen spreads disease and disaster in the body. Semen is the atomic energy in man. One spermatozoa is capable of producing one human being, while three million are lost at one ejaculation. Use this energy in a judicious manner. Animals and plants are more wise in sexual matters. They do sex only in a particular season. Sex energy can be transmuted for higher creative purposes. Waste of semen is the waste of a vital life force.

15. *Sexual enjoyment is the lowest short lived ecstasy.*

16. *Fighting with the sexual desires dissipate more energy than indulging in sex.*

17. *Pleasure in sex comes from the mind and not from the sexual organs. Sexual organs are only the mediums and not the means. Those organs obey the commands of the mind. When one realises this, sex stops troubling. Mind should be controlled and disciplined to subdue the superfluous sex desires.*

18. *Lord Jesus says—If you have lustful look, you have already committed adultery in your heart.*

19. *Your wife is your companion, co-worker and equal partner in life's struggle. Don't treat her just as an instrument of sexual gratification or as a domestic servant.*

20. *Very few people march straight to success without going through periods of temporary failures and discouragements. These are the part and parcel of human life.*

21. *Money can buy many things and can produce wealth. But money can't buy or produce peace of mind. Peace of mind is more valuable than money or wealth.*

22. *Do as you wish to be done by is the golden rule in human relations.*

23. *Happiness is contagious in nature. It comes back when you share happiness with others without any selfish motive.*

24. *Unpeaceful thoughts always make the people sick.*

25. *Muscle tension is caused due to mental tension. When mental tension is removed, muscle tension also ceases.*

26. *When we control our emotions we gain power. But when emotions control us the results are often disastrous.*

27. *To have peace of mind discipline yourself never to get mad or resentful.*

28. *Don't become a grievance collector. It will surely destroy your own peace of mind.*

29. *Fatigue is not caused by work or over-work, but by hurry, worry, tension, anxiety and grudges.*

30. *When you think tiredness you start feeling tired, when you think energy you feel alive. Therefore avoid growing tired in your thoughts and attitude. Keep your eagerness and interest in every aspect of life at a high level. You will start feeling new energy in your body and mind.*

31. *When you go to sleep don't bother about your plans for the next day.*

32. *God who has helped you so far, will help you tomorrow also.*

33. *Worry is a live grave. By avoiding worry we can live longer and better.*

34. *Fear is one of the main causes of many troubles in the world. Fear often owes its existence to some old vague memory and has no present substance.*

35. *Your mind can transmute your fear into a real susbstance. When you fear something, that thing is more likely to find you and harm you.*

36. *If you do not know the method of relaxation, you are slow poisoning your body.*

37. *Worry, tension, stress, strain and hurry are killing the people like flies.*

38. *Don't be afraid of criticism. Try to improve yourself in the light of criticism. Go ahead, no matter who criticizes.*

39. *It is not good to go on searching for symptoms of any imaginary illness. If you will imagine illness, fear illness, you will surely bring illness upon yourself. Mind can transmute your belief into its physical equivalent.*

40. *Many psychosomatic diseases are caused due to unpeace of mind.*

41. *Faith has a very strange power of curing even incurable diseases.*

42. *Nature never takes away anything without replacing with something of equal potential value.*

43. *Look at your problem in a creative and positive manner and you will find bright opportunities which you have not*

thought of. Never think negative. Be realistic, face all the facts, but always look on the hopeful side.

44. Before you could win, you had to learn to lose.

45. When you do something helpful for another person you always feel better. It is the secret of happiness.

46. Enthusiasm and eagerness can make any job thrilling. Love your job. If you do not like it now, learn to like it.

47. Don't take yourself too damn seriously, unless you wish to be damned by others.

48. Lack of money also destroys peace of mind. If you have mastered money you may have peace of mind. If money has mastered you, then you won't have peace of mind. You can be rich with peace of mind. But you can't be rich without peace of mind.

49. Money can buy many things but not peace of mind, but can surely help you to find peace of mind.

50. Nobody who goes too deeply into debt can get peace of mind.

51. The more you give of what you have, the more comes back to you. It is the law of the nature.

52. When you share your blessings with others, you become his creditor. Eventually the debt is paid. Somehow, debts have to be paid.

53. Wealth is not something you grab from others, it is something you build for yourself out of service to others.

54. The motives of love, sex and money rule the world.

55. When you have peace of mind at home you can count on having peace of mind everywhere.

56. Your own mental attitude can make you peaceful or unpeaceful. Control your mental attitude. Negative attitude will lead you towards miseries and positive attitude will lead you towards happiness. A positive mind automatically obtains benefits from other positive minds.

57. A man who works wholeheartedly at his job is not concerned with such matters as finding faults with others.

58. *Many successful men do not possess any greater intelligence than most other men possess. Yet their achievements are very high due to their positive mental attitude which makes their brain-power more efficient.*

59. *Great men have no time to waste with a desire to injure others. If they did, they would not be great men.*

60. *Fear and anger put the mind behind bars. Guilt wraps the mind in chains.*

61. *When you befool anybody with clever words, you befool yourself also.*

62. *One who makes his money through taking dishonest advantage of his fellow men, has cheated himself of the genuine joy which comes with honest success.*

63. *When you obey the rules of the game, and win, you have done something for your soul. When you cheat and win, you only call it winning. But you have really lost instead.*

64. *Stress is the cause of many diseases. In this hurry up world we are subjecting ourselves to too many stresses.*

65. *Learn to live also. You are learning only how to get rich.*

66. *Never remain angry. Begin each day by liking everyone you meet.*

67. *Never go to bed angry with your wife.*

68. *Ill will is also the cause of ill health.*

69. *Whatever your mind believes can also achieve.*

70. *Lack of confidence in oneself is one of the greatest barriers to the full expression of your personality.*

71. *Until you are willing to be your own self at your own level, you can not know yourself, nor know what your mind can accomplish. Nobody can be anyone else without harming his own personality.*

72. *Peace of mind is the peaceful base upon which we can erect a good deal of life dynamic.*

73. *A person who is his own master, never seeks revenge on anyone. Revenge can be spuriously sweet, but it is a sweet*

poison to the personality.

74. *A major reason for unhappiness is the tendency to meddle with the lives of others while we take too little time in trying to improve ourselves.*

75. *If you compromise yourself with your own conscience, you will weaken your conscience. Soon your conscience will fail to guide you, and you never will have real wealth based on peace of mind.*

76. *Worry is the biggest problem facing mankind. It destroys our ability*
   to concentrate. When we worry our mind jumps here and there and everywhere. We lose our power of decision making.

77. *When we force ourselves to face the worst and accept it mentally, we then eliminate all these vague imaginings and put ourselves in a position in which we are able to concentrate on our problem.*

78. *According to Dr. Alexis Carrel—"Those who do not know how to fight worry, die young."*

79. *Most of the patients who come to physicians could cure themselves if they only get rid of their anger, fear, worries, hate, selfishness and their inability to adjust themselves to the world of reality.*

80. *Many businessmen are wrecking their bodies with heart diseases, ulcers and high blood pressure due to hurry and worry, stress and strain.*

81. *Always remember even if you are able to acquire the whole world, you could sleep only in one bed at a time and eat only three meals a day, which even an ordinary person can easily do.*

82. *Nervous troubles are caused by emotions of futility, frustration, anxiety, worry, fear, defeat and despair etc.*

83. *The main causes of insanity are worry and fear.*

84. *According to Alexis Carrel—"Those who keep the peace of their inner selves in the midst of the tumult of the modern*

city are immune to nervous diseases".

85. *According to the American Dental Association—"Unpleasant emotions such as those caused by worry, fear and nagging. . . may upset the body's calcium balance and cause tooth decay."*

86. *According to William James—"The Lord may forgive our sins, but the nervous system never does."*

87. *A cheerful mental attitude helps the body to fight diseases.*

88. *Many worries are caused due to making decisions before they have sufficient knowledge on which to base decision.*

89. *Trivialities are at the bottom of most of our marital unhappiness. We allow ourselves to be upset by small things we should despise and forget.*

90. *Nearly all of our worries and unhappiness come from our imagination and not from reality. We worry about things that rarely happen.*

91. *Don't worry about those things which are beyond your power and leave them to the will of God. It is useless to fight with the inevitable.*

92. *According to Marcus Aurelius—"Our life is what our thoughts make it." Happy thoughts make us happy and miserable thoughts make us miserable.*

93. *When we hate our enemies, we are giving them power over our sleep, our appetite. Hatred destroys our ability to enjoy even our food. It increases our Blood Pressure and affects our health and happiness.*

94. *If you have a weak heart, then even one fit of anger can kill you.*

95. *If you can't love your enemies, then atleast forgive them and forget them for the sake of your own health.*

96. *According to Epictetus—"Every man will pay the penalty for his own misdeeds. The man who remembers this will be angry with no one, indignant with no one, revile no one, offend no one and hate no one".*

97. According to Lincoln—"All of us are the children of conditions, of circumstances, of environment, of education, of acquired habits and of heredity moulding men as they are and will forever be.

98. It is natural to forget to be grateful. So, it is folly to expect gratitude for any of our work. If you want to enjoy happiness, stop thinking about gratitude or ingratitude. Do work only for the inner joy of giving.

99. Those who do not teach their children to express gratitude, they should not expect gratitude from them. To raise grateful children, we have to be grateful ourselves. Don't belittle the kindness of others in the presence of your children.

100. Most of the things in our lives are right and only a few are wrong. To keep oneself happy try to concentrate on right things and avoid wrong things. But if you want unhappiness then concentrate on wrong things and avoid right things.

101. Think of all we have to be grateful for and thank God for all our boons and bounties.

102. According to Jonathan Swift, author of Gulliver's Travels—"The best doctors in the world are—Doctor Diet, Doctor Quiet, and Doctor Merryman".

103. Never do anything you don't like yourself.

104. According to Prophet Mohammed—"Do a good deed everyday. A good deed is one that brings a smile of joy to the face of another."
When we try to please others, it causes us to stop thinking about ourselves. And this saves us from worry, fear and melancholy.

105. Religious life helps us to protect ourselves from ulcer, angina pectoris, nervous breakdown, and insanity.

106. According to Dr. Carrel—"Prayer is the most powerful form of energy one can generate. When we pray, we link ourselves with the inexhaustible motive power that spins

the universe. Whenever we address God in fervent prayer, we change both soul and body for the better. It helps us to put into words exactly what is troubling us and gives us relief."

107. In every person there are deep wells of hidden strength that are never found and used. Yogis awaken their Kundalini to arouse that sleeping power and utilize that power for spiritual progress.

108. Vulgar people always feel happy when they criticize others. Don't bother about your unjust criticism. It may prove a blessing in disguise for you.

109. Most of our fatigue is caused due to our mental and emotional attitude. Boredom, resentment, a feeling of not being appreciated, a feeling of futility, hurry, worry and anxiety like emotional factors cause fatigue.

110. If you don't find happiness in your work, you may never find it anywhere. Getting interested in your job will take your mind off your worries.

111. No one ever died due to lack of sleep. Nature itself takes care of your necessary sleep. Worrying about insomnia causes more damage than sleeplessness itself.

112. Those who don't know how to relax their bodies and minds are committing slow suicide.

113. Many divorces are caused due to lack of proper sexual knowledge by either of the partners. It would be better to read any good book on sex to avoid sex related troubles.

114. Everybody wants appreciation and recognition. They are ready to do anything to get it.

115. Accumulation mania is at the opposite pole from a mind that knows peace. Rich men are always filled with hatred and mistrust. Their worst hatred is directed towards the Government. They prophecy that the Government could cause them to die as a pauper.

116. Rest or sleep taken in the early afternoon (siesta) after lunch provides relaxation to body and mind.

SELF-IMPROVEMENT/PERSONALITY DEVELOPMENT

Also Available
in Hindi

Also Available
in Hindi

Also Available
in Kannada, Tamil

Also Available
in Kannada

Also Available
in Kannada

All books available at www.vspublishers.com

Also Available
in Hindi, Kannada

Also Available
in Hindi, Kannada

Contact us at sales@vspublishers.com

QUIZ BOOKS

ENGLISH IMPROVEMENT

ACTIVITIES BOOK

QUOTES/SAYINGS

BIOGRAPHIES

CHILDREN SCIENCE LIBRARY

Set Code: 02122 S

Set Code: 12138 S

IELTS TECH

COMPUTER BOOKS

Also available in Hindi

Also available in Hindi

All books available at www.vspublishers.com